sweetness &lightning

1

Gido Amagakure

c o n t e n t s

MORNING, DADDY!

BEEP

BEEP BEEP BEEP...

MMM...

JERK

SFFF...

DON'T MOVE...

GURGLE GURGLE GURGLE GURGLE

HUH?

HEY! TSUMUGI! YOU'RE STEPPING ON THE HANDOUTS!

CLK CRINKLE

NGH.

S'MORNING!

CRINKLE

Chapter 1 | Uniforms and Donabe Rice

OKAY!

SMACK

SMACK

YES, SIR!

WATCH IT WHILE YOU EAT BREAKFAST.

SURE, SURE.

DADDY, CAN I WATCH MAGI-GAL?

I CAN'T FIND MY PINK MAGI-GAL OUTFIT!

HOLD ON A SECOND.

DADDY!

I GOTTA BUY CHERRY TOMATOES...

PLUCK

PLUCK

LOOKS LIKE YOUR REMARK WAS OFF THE MARK!

TRA LA LA

DING

PACKAGES: FROZEN EDAMAME, FRIED CHICKEN
LEFT: JELLY

8

LOOK HOW THIN HE'S GETTING, THOUGH!

SCRAWNY

HIS DAUGHTER'S STILL LITTLE, YOU KNOW?

HE KIND OF HAS TO.

Huh... THAT'S A SHAME.

And it's at a bar...

I THINK WE NEED TO FILL THAT BELLY OF HIS.

FLIP

I'VE ALSO TRIED COOKING ONCE, BUT...

I'VE NEVER BEEN A BIG EATER.

DON'T WORRY ABOUT ME.

MOMOYA-SENSEI, THAT'S REALLY NONE OF YOUR BUSINESS.

Well, LATELY, EVEN THE CONVENIENCE STORE BOXED LUNCHES HAVE THE RIGHT AMOUNT OF CALORIES AND NUTRITION.

BWA-HA!

That's sooo cute!

...IT CAUSED MY DAUGHTER TO MAKE A FACE I'D NEVER SEEN BEFORE.

YEAH. IT'S A BIG HELP.

Hey!

TSUMUGI, YOU STARTLED HER!

Oh...

NO, I'M FINE.

HUH?

ARE YOU OKAY?

FLIP くる スタッ TMP

I'M CRYING BECAUSE THIS FOOD IS DELICIOUS.

IT MEANS SHE DIDN'T COME.

YUP!

WHEN DID SHE LEARN THAT?

DO YOU KNOW WHAT THAT MEANS?

MY MOM PROMISED TO MEET ME, BUT SHE FLAKED...

I ATE IT ALL, THOUGH!

THIS WASN'T JUST FOR ME. IT WAS ORIGINALLY MEANT FOR TWO PEOPLE.

CLACK

I SEE.

UM, I MEAN...

I'M NOT CRYING BECAUSE I'M LONELY.

HUH?

AND SO... ...I GOT MAD.

BUT THE FOOD WAS GOOD, EVEN IF I WAS ALONE.

SO I STARTED THINKING ABOUT HOW SHE MADE IT.

I KNOW SHE'S BUSY...

I SEE.

AS I ATE, I JUST KEPT REMEMBERING THINGS...

...AND THEN...

...I STARTED CRYING, FOR SOME REASON.

Uh...

YOU ATE IT ALL BY YOURSELF?

...SORRY, IT'S ALL GONE.

YES, I ATE IT ALL BY MYSELF!

WAS IT THAT GOOD?

DROOL

MY NAME IS KOTORI IIDA.

HERE.

Oh

WELL...

IF YOU WANT...

RUSTLE

COME BY SOMETIME AND TRY THE FOOD.

THIS IS MY MOM'S RESTAURANT.

CARD: MEGUMI RESTAURANT

SIGN: DRAGON HOT BENTO (BOXED LUNCH)

IT'S A LITTLE EARLY...

...BUT LET'S GET SOMETHING TO EAT AND GO HOME.

NOPE!

HEH HEH...

SQUEEZE

...

YOU DON'T WANT ONE? WOULD YOU RATHER EAT OUT?

BOXED LUNCHES AGAIN?

The light of hooope!

Magical! Magi-Gal!

HUP!

RUSTLE

SHOVE

I'LL TALK TO MOM...

Nah... I WANT TO DO AS MUCH AS I CAN ON MY OWN.

I THINK WE NEED TO START EATING MEALS AT HOME.

THE WIND WAS STRONG TODAY.

WE WERE LUCKY THERE WERE STILL SOME CHERRY BLOSSOMS LEFT.

KA-SHH

CLUNK

...

SORRY! THE SITTER ALREADY LEFT, RIGHT?

I'M BACK!

KA-CHAK

THE

LIGHT

OF

HOPE...

CLATTER

UM...

YOU'RE THE GIRL FROM BEFORE?

She's prettier than I remember—

YES, THAT'S RIGHT.

NICE TO SEE YOU AGAIN.

SHE'S OUT HELPING SOMEONE WHO'S DONE A LOT FOR US...

MY MOM IS...WELL...

MUMBLE

I DON'T REALLY EAT A LOT...

...AND I DON'T KNOW WHAT'S POPULAR.

I...

I SEE...

GLOOM

...BUT YOU CAN'T ASK ME TO GIVE YOU THE NAME OF ONE OF OUR RIVALS!

SURE, MY MOTHER ISN'T HERE...

No...

...that's not...

...what I meant...

WE'RE THE BEST AROUND HERE!

IS THERE ANYPLACE GOOD AROUND HERE?

DONABE

...COOK SOME RICE, YOU KNOW!

I...

I CAN AT LEAST...

PLEASE TAKE A SEAT!

GO AHEAD!

Uh...

UM...

IT'S SUPER-GOOD!

It's a clay pot, 'kay?

A NABE POT!

IS RICE FROM A POT GOOD?

27

SWISH

Mm.

...

WHEW...

POOPIES?

No!

DADDY'S GONNA GO TO THE BATH-ROOM.

...

UM...

PARDON ME FOR A MOMENT.

Oh

SURE.

UGH, MOMMM!

?!

C'MON, HELP ME...

MUMBLE

MUMBLE

MUMBLE

?

WHAT'S A CUP? HOW MUCH IS IT? IF YOU HEAR THIS MESSAGE, PLEASE GIVE ME A CALL!

WHY DON'T DONABE HAVE THE MARKS ON THE INSIDE FOR COOKING RICE? I TRIED TO BE COOL AND SAID I COULD MAKE IT!

...ARE YOU OKAY?

DIGNIFIED

SORRY TO KEEP YOU WAITING.

WHY WOULD I NOT BE?

SNEAK

DID YOU POOPIES?

I'M BACK...

NO, AND I COULDN'T GO, ANY-WAYS.

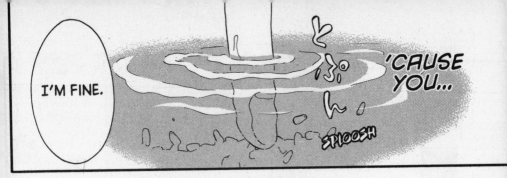

I'M FINE.

'CAUSE YOU...

SPLOOSH

...YOU CAN'T COOK, CAN YOU?

WHEN I WENT CAMPING, THIS IS HOW WE MEASURED THE WATER.

THAT'S FOR COOKING RICE OVER A CAMP-FIRE...

WE EAT ALL THE TIME.

IT'S BEEN A LONG TIME SINCE WE'VE EATEN!

Thanks!

Sure. Use this.

OR SHOULD I GO TO AN-OTHER RESTAU-RANT?

MAY-BE I SHOULD GO HOME.

Uhhh...

YOU NEED TO LET IT... ABSORB THE WATER, SO GIVE IT A MINUTE.

I'M GONNA DRAW WHILE WE WAIT!

FWIP

Hff

UM...

I MEAN TOGETHER, DADDY.

OH...

YOU MIGHT BE RIGHT...

YEAH...

THAT SHOULD BE ENOUGH TIME...I THINK.

FWOOM

ボォ...

Umm...

SAKE!

I'VE HEARD IT TASTES BETTER IF YOU MIX IN A LITTLE SAKE.

I'M SURE OF IT.

ホ"

MUMBLE

BLUP

ト"ト"

ト"

BLUP

I'm nervous.

BEEP!

14 59

分

—リセット—

RESET

秒

START/STOP

スタート

KA-POP

Huh?

WAS I ASLEEP?

Yawn

BEEP
BEEP
BEEP
BEEP

TWITCH

WHUSH

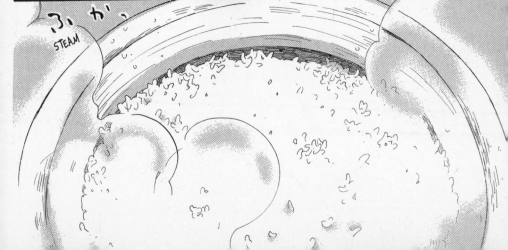

STEAM

PILE 'EM ON AND LET'S EAT!

MORE FOOD? MORE FOOD?

Sec- onds

I FOUND SOME PICKLED NOZAWANA AND MISO BEEF AND IWANORI SEAWEED!

OH!

O-OH!

UM...

TOPPINGS!

CLATTER

I PROMISE YOU...

TSU-MUGI.

HMM?

MUNCH

MUNCH

Oh...

YES.

THANK YOU.

W-

WAS MY RICE GOOD?

YES?

UM, INU-ZUKA-SENSEI...

I WANTED TO ASK YOU SOMETHING.

SENSEI?

Hm?

SO...

...EATING DINNER ALONE MOST OF THE TIME FROM NOW ON.

I'M...

I'M GOING TO BE...

Chapter 1 – END

DONABE RICE

☆ Ingredients ☆ Serves 3-4

1 1/2 cups rice

Ooh! 430 mL water – Try to have between 1.2 and 1.3 times as much water as rice.

A dash of sake

Steps

1. Wash the **rice**, then pour it and the **water** into the donabe. Cover and heat on medium high. When it seems ready to boil over, turn the heat to low and cook for 13 minutes.

+POINT+
Add a bit of flavor by putting in a little **sake**.

2. Turn the heat to high for 30 seconds, then turn off the heat and let it steam for ten minutes. Remove the lid and stir.

~POINT~
You can adjust the amount of water and the heat settings to your taste.

Try it once you get used to the recipe!

How to clean rice to make it delicious

Quickly!

1. Put the **rice** in a metal strainer. Soak the whole thing in a bowl filled with water. Stir the rice around with your hands and then lift it out of the water.

2. Continue to stir the **rice** without putting it back into the water. Stir it quickly but gently.

3. Get a fresh bowl of water and soak/mix again. Make sure the rice bran is getting rinsed off. Strain and stir. Repeat.

4. When the water no longer clouds up, strain the rice and let it sit for 30 minutes in the summer or an hour in the winter (to absorb the moisture).

I love rice!

Huh? You left it in the water the whole time...

Let's try it next time!

This lets the rice fully aborb the water it's been soaked in.

CONVERSION NOTES:
430 ML WATER = ABOUT 1 3/4 CUPS

Chapter 2 | Pork Miso Soup and Restaurant Lights

AND I LIKE THIS ONE, TOO! IT'S SOFT AND YUMMY AND ROUND AND CUTE!

THIS ONE'S GOT AN ANIMAL PICTURE ON THE INSIDE, AND IT'S YUMMY.

THE REST ARE SO-SO.

I SEE. THEN I'LL SEAL AWAY THE REST OF THEM.

OH, RIGHT. TSUMUGI!

ARE THERE ANY OF THESE YOU LIKE?

FOR BOXED LUNCHES?

PACKAGES: (L) EDAMAME VEGGIE MIX; (R) SHRIMP MACARONI CORN GRATIN, HOROSCOPE INCLUDED.

...THAT HE'D DO HIS BEST TO COOK FOR YOU, RIGHT?

DADDY PROMISED YOU...

THAT'S WHY.

SEAL THEM AWAY? WHY?

FOOD...

WELL...

MAYBE NOT...

I was thinking of taking a cooking class...

WITH KOTORI-CHAN TOO?!

COULD
WE COOK
AND EAT
TOGETHER?

HUH?

WHY?

IT'S NOT ABOUT WHETHER I WANT TO OR NOT. I JUST CAN'T.

DO YOU NOT WANT TO?

EATING DINNER WITH SOME RANDOM GUY AND HIS KID?

THAT'S NOT THE ISSUE!

THAT'S NOT TRUE!

I'LL TALK TO MY MOM ABOUT IT!

FOR ONE THING, WHY WOULD WE...

WHAT WHAT?

WHAT?

WHAT WHAT WHAT WHAT WHAAAT?

I DOUBT YOUR MOTHER WOULD BE OKAY WITH THAT. WE'D BE A BOTHER.

TSU-

TSUMUGI, WAIT.

I WANT US TO ALL EAT HERE TOGETHER AGAIN.

REALLY?!

IT'S LIKE A RESTAURANT!

I WANNA DO THAT!

WHY? WHY WHY?

"OH, JEEZ..."

NO, NOT EVEN IF YOU MAKE A CUTE FACE!

...

SO...

...THE RESTAURANT'S CLOSED A LOT, ANYWAY.

MY MOM WILL BE FINE, REALLY.

SHE'S BUSY WITH OTHER WORK NOW.

IT FEELS...

...LIKE THE RESTAURANT MIGHT SHUT DOWN.

...

IT DOESN'T HAVE TO BE EVERY DAY.

I DON'T HAVE A DAD...

...SO THERE'S NOBODY ELSE I CAN RELY ON.

JUST COME HERE ONCE IN A WHILE...

...TURN ON THE LIGHTS...

...AND MAKE SOMETHING TO EAT WITH ME.

HUH?

MY MOM WILL BE FINE WITH IT SINCE YOU'RE A TEACHER!

AND IT'S NOT LIKE WE DON'T KNOW YOU.

SO YOU ARE FROM MY SCHOOL...

YES.

KOTORI IIDA, CLASS 1-A.

YOU'RE MY ASSISTANT HOMEROOM TEACHER.

HAVE YOU STILL NOT LEARNED THE NAMES OF YOUR STUDENTS?

UHH...

I'LL.... GO HOME AND THINK ABOUT IT.

DONG

DING

CLACK

FWIP

WHO CAN SOLVE THIS PROB-LEM?

OKAY.

YOU DON'T WANT PEOPLE TO FIND OUT THAT YOU'RE MEETING WITH A FEMALE STUDENT OUTSIDE SCHOOL.

I UNDERSTAND, SENSEI.

WHAT IF HE FALLS IN LOVE WITH ME?

GASP!

EATING HER SECOND BREAKFAST

MUNCH

MUNCH

I'LL PRETEND I DON'T KNOW ANYTHING SO PEOPLE DON'T MIS-UNDERSTAND.

?

SHAKE

SHAKE

BLUSH

...

IT WOULD BE BAD, RIGHT?

GOING TO A SPECIFIC STUDENT'S HOUSE...

I SEE.

HM... KOTORI IIDA, HUH?

HER DAD DIVORCED HER MOM WHEN SHE WAS IN THIRD GRADE.

HOMEROOM TEACHER: HOSAKA

BUT WHEN I WAS YOUNG, I WOULD GO HANG OUT WITH THE STUDENTS AND EAT AT THEIR HOUSES.

WELL...

...PEOPLE ARE MORE PARTICULAR ABOUT THAT LATELY.

SO NOT MANY TEACHERS INTERACT WITH STUDENTS OUTSIDE OF CLASS THESE DAYS.

WELL, IF YOU'RE TALKING TO ME ABOUT IT, YOU MUST NOT BE SURE WHAT TO DO.

PART OF YOU WANTS TO DO IT, RIGHT?

HM...

Then you go, Sensei.

Nope. She's asking for you, right?

TRY TALKING WITH HER MOM. JUST ONCE.

WHETHER IT'S FOR YOUR LITTLE GIRL'S SAKE, OR FOR YOUR SAKE...

SHE CAN HELP YOU DECIDE WHAT TO DO.

54

THIS WAY...

...I THINK.

DA·DUN!

THANK YOU.
MY MOM WILL BE HERE
WEDNESDAY NIGHT.
PLEASE EAT WITH US.
AND BRING TSUMUGI-
CHAN!

CLASS 1-A
KOTORI IIDA

THAT WAS FAST.

CLATTER

EXCUSE ME...

THAT'S IT!

...SHE HAD TO LEAVE SUDDENLY FOR WORK.

She was here until this afternoon, but...

Wait a second!

WHERE'S YOUR MOM?

IT'S TRUE! I HAVE A LETTER AND EVERYTHING!

WOW...

EXTREMELY SORRY

Dear Inuzuka-sensei,

This is Kotori's mother. I'm very grateful that you're going to be looking after my daughter. Use the kitchen however you want. I'm sorry, but I have to leave suddenly for work. Thank you very much.

AND I HAD HER PUT HER THUMB-PRINT ON IT, TOO!

DON'T WORRY.

I HAD HER WRITE DOWN THE RECIPE FOR ME.

THE PLAN WAS FOR YOUR MOM TO MAKE US SALISBURY STEAK FROM SCRATCH, BUT...

WHAT SHOULD WE DO?

OKAY, THEN.

SALISB...

♡It's easy

Step 1 Slice up the onions into tiny bits!!

You'll cry a bit.

Cook until they change color.

Cooking ya!

SUPER-SIMPLE

LET ME SEE.

Hm?

OH.

FROM THE LOOKS OF IT...

...SO SHE MADE IT KIND OF KID-FRIENDLY.

I TOLD HER THERE'D BE A LITTLE GIRL COMING...

IS THIS A PICTURE BOOK?

IF WE COULD AT LEAST DO THE SALISBURY STEAK...

THAT WAS TSUMUGI-CHAN'S REQUEST, WASN'T IT?

YOU REALLY DON'T EAT A LOT, SENSEI.

I see that now.

WHAT ?!

...ALSO, WE CAN'T POSSIBLY EAT ALL THIS.

MENU
○ Rice
○ Miso Soup (Po...
○ Salisbury Steak with egg
○ ...mato and Veggie Salad
○ ...Dressing
○ ...Potatoes
○ ...ce Cream

A menu featuring everybody's requests.

SO...

YOU CAN'T COOK EITHER, RIGHT?

OR SO I'VE HEARD.

SWF

...WHY DON'T YOU CUT THEM WITH ME?

I'M...

...THE TASTE TESTER.

I...

OKAY...

...THAT'S
FINE.

...

DID I
ASK
HER IN
A BAD
WAY?

CHOP

HOW
is it?

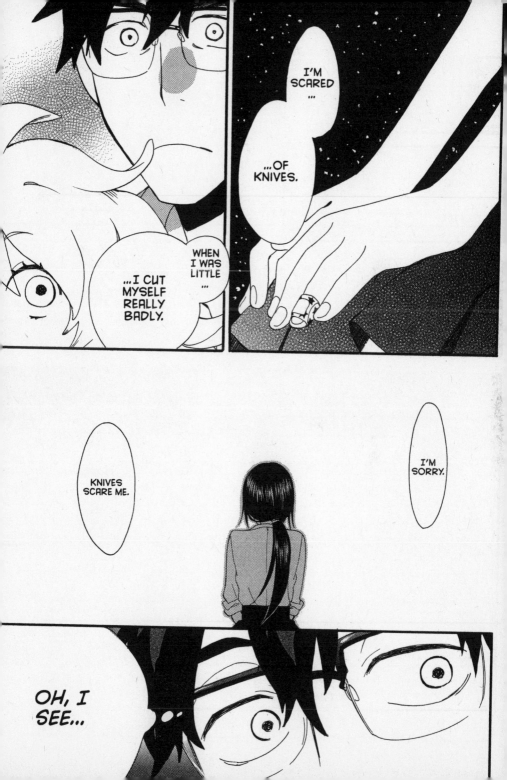

SO YOU WANTED SOMEONE TO DO THE CUTTING FOR YOU?

Unngh

...

YES.

YOU WERE HAVING TROUBLE, AND I LIKE TO EAT, AND I CAN BE A TASTE TESTER...

I THOUGHT IT WAS A REALLY GOOD IDEA, BUT..

I WISH I COULD DO IT.

MY MOM'S ALWAYS BUSY, AND I KNOW IT WOULD HELP HER.

BUT I JUST CAN'T.

ACTUALLY, I FEEL BETTER NOW THAT I KNOW WHAT YOU WERE THINKING.

...?

OH.

NO.

BUT IT LOOKS LIKE I WAS...

I'M SORRY I DIDN'T TELL YOU.

I WASN'T TRYING TO USE YOU OR ANYTHING.

I WAS REALLY IN A BIND.

I DIDN'T KNOW IF I COULD MAKE GOOD FOOD FOR TSUMUGI BY MYSELF.

IT'S TOUGH.

FOR BOTH OF US...

SO IN A WAY...

...COOKING TOGETHER IS GOOD FOR BOTH OF US.

...AND WHEN WE SAW THE LIGHTS ON HERE, WE FELT SO RELIEVED.

I KNOW YOU DON'T WANT THE RESTAURANT TO CLOSE...

DADDY! MAKE IT THINNER!

SURE THING.

IS IT STILL A LITTLE TOO TOUGH?

GRRRR

Uuuugh... this carrot...

LET'S PARBOIL IT.

WHAT ABOUT THE MEAT?

IT BRINGS OUT THE FLAVOR.

...OR SO I'VE HEARD.

YOU BOIL THE WATER FIRST, RIGHT?

PAPER: TSU TSU TSU... MU MU MU... *TABLE: KOTORI IIDA*

YES...

WILL YOU HELP ME?

FOR TSU-MUGI, TOO.

...BUT I LIKE ADDING THE FLAVOR LITTLE BY LITTLE.

IT'S FINE TO LEARN TO PUT IN A SPECIFIC AMOUNT...

SOME PREFER MILD ONES.

SOME PEOPLE LIKE STRONG FLAVORS.

JAR: MISO

HOW IS IT?

I LIKE ABOUT THIS MUCH!

Heh heh

...

YOU LEARNED YOUR MOTHER'S WAY OF SEASONING, HUH?

71

...IT'S DELI-CIOUS.

BA-DUM

BA-DUM

BA-DUM

SSSLURP

PUFF

PUFF

PUFF

Let's eaaat!

72

I'M FINE.

I'M JUST SO INCREDIBLY HAPPY, YOU KNOW?

YEAH ...

RIGHT? SO HOT AND TASTY! TARO ARE BEST IN WINTER, BUT I ALSO LIKE YAMS AND SWEET POTATOES.

CHOMP

THE POTATOES ARE PRETTY GOOD.

Look, my star!

THE PO'A'OES AH HA'!

Hmpwh!

IT'S HA'!

PUFF

BLOW ON THEM.

PUFF

BUT WE RAN OUT OF ENERGY AND NEVER MADE THE SALISBURY STEAK...

I'm glad the rice was done in time.

Sorry.

Sweet! Yummy yummy!

HAPPY

Ahh... BUT RICE AND PORK MISO SOUP...

...GO TOGETHER SO WONDERFULLY.

LOOKING FORWARD TO NEXT TIME!

YEAH!

Hee hee!

LET'S DO SALISBURY STEAK NEXT TIME! SALISBURY STEAK AND RICE OMELETTES, AND THAT MEATBALL THING WOULD BE GOOD, TOO!

...OKAY.

WE'LL BE LEAVING AT EIGHT.

I NEED TO GET TSUMUGI READY FOR BED.

...

YOU TOO, KOTORI-CHAN!

...

I...

PAPER: SEA, SQUID

Chapter 2 - END

MISO PORK SOUP

☆ Ingredients ☆ Serves 3-4

7 cm daikon radish
1/2 carrot
1/2 green onion
1/3 burdock root
1 potato
150 g pork (brisket)

1/2 block konnyaku
9 snow pea pods
1 pouch fried tofu
1 Tbsp sesame oil
800 mL dashi stock
4 Tbsp miso

We use pork butt at our house.

A bunch!

Steps

Hmm...
Hmm...

1. Cut the **carrots** and **daikon radish** into quarter rounds, then cut the **green onion** into 1 cm slices. Chop the **burdock root** in thin diagonal slices and place in cold water. Cut the **potatoes** and **pork** into bite-sized pieces. Tear the **konnyaku** into bite-sized chunks and then parboil. Parboil the **snow peas** and the **fried tofu**. Drain.

Then cut them up!

2. Put the **sesame oil** into the pot and stir-fry the **pork** on medium heat. Add and fry the ingredients in this order: **carrots, burdock root, daikon radish, potatoes, konnyaku.** Once the edges of the **potatoes** become translucent, add in the **dashi stock**.

☆POINT☆
You can boil the ingredients instead of frying. The taste will be lighter.

3. Once it starts boiling, skim off the scum that forms on top. Simmer on low heat for 7-8 minutes, then add the **green onion** and **fried tofu**.

4. Once the ingredients are softened, add the **miso** by dissolving it gradually into the stock. Once it starts boiling again, immediately turn off the heat and add the **snow peas**.

It's important to taste-test!

CONVERSION NOTES:
7 CM DAIKON ≈ 3 IN., 150 G PORK ≈ ABOUT 5 1/4 OZ, 800 ML DASHI ≈ ABOUT 3 1/3 CUPS

Hnn...

BEEP BEEP BEEP ピ
ピ ピ ピ ピ
BEEP

STEP
STEP
STEP

CLick

STEP

mumble

mumble

MORNING
...

CLICK

SILENCE

STEP

WOW! MY FRIED TOFU IS SO LONG!

DANGLE

HOW'S THE MISO SOUP? I ACCIDENTALLY BOILED IT A LITTLE...

YOURS IS ALL BURNT, DADDY!

BUT I FLAVORED IT LIKE WE DID WITH THE PORK MISO SOUP...

I HAVE TO PAY FOR MY MISTAKES.

CONGRATULATIONS.

Let's look at the weather...

BEEP

REALLY?! IS THAT A THING?!

THAT MEANS YOU, UH...

...WON, TSUMUGI.

BEEP

FLICK

A LIVE BROADCAST?

Good morning, mommy's got a live broadcast at 7:15 this morning! I'm nervous... Have a good victory!

RUSTLE

HM?

What's this?

7:15...?

Huh?

RIGHT NOW?

82

...AND MY MOM WAS WEARING A SAILOR UNIFORM.

I TURNED ON THE TV IN THE MORNING...

CHOMP

EVEN IF IT IS FOR TV, THERE ARE SOME THINGS YOU SHOULDN'T DO!

NO WAY.

I MEAN, JUST, NO WAY!

CHOMP

SO IS THIS WHY YOUR MOM IS BUSY?

YEAH.

IT'S NOT LIKE SHE'S REALLY BECOME A CELEBRITY, THOUGH.

IS THAT THE PROBLEM?

I'VE NEVER EVEN WORN A SAILOR UNIFORM!

And it looked great on her.

BOX: TSUMUGI INUZUKA, CLAY

TSU-MUGI!

THERE'S BEEN A LITTLE TROUBLE WITH MY DAUGHTER.

Oh, gotcha.

Sure. Get going.

I'll tell the vice-principal.

SO, UH...

TSUMUGI AND MIKIO-KUN ARE...

INUZUKA-SAN, SORRY TO CALL YOU LIKE THIS.

NO, IT'S OKAY. THANK YOU.

TSU...

I DID NOT!

TSUMUGI-CHAN SCRATCHED ME!

A tiny bit.

...OVER THERE.

NO!

TSUMUGI-CHAN, LISTEN...

UM. TSU-MUGI, MIKIO-KUN IS SAYING HE'S...

NO WAY!

NEVER!!

BOW

See you!

Bye bye, Tsumugi-chan!

SORRY. CAN I TAKE HER HOME AND TALK WITH HER?

YEAH.

...

DING

VNNN

IT'S JUST DADDY NOW.

HEY, TSU-MUGI.

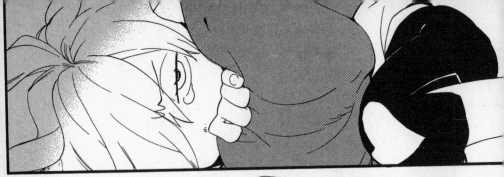

YEAH.

HE SAID A MEAN THING TO YOU, DIDN'T HE?

I KNOW. YOU'RE NOT A THIEF, TSUMUGI.

THEY GAVE ME THE CLAY...

I'M NOT A THIEF.

...

...OKAY.

THERE, THERE.

PAT
PAT

DADDY DOESN'T WANT YOU TO BE CALLED A THIEF, EITHER, EVEN IF IT'S A MISUNDERSTANDING.

TO SORT THINGS OUT.

WHY?

HEY. WHY DON'T WE BUY SOME CLAY AT HOME SO YOU CAN GIVE THEIRS BACK?

THERE ARE FEWER INGREDIENTS IN THIS THAN I THOUGHT.

...YOU SOAK THE BREAD-CRUMBS IN MILK?

SO...

HUH...

Then again...

SOME PEOPLE PUT SOY PULP OR TOFU OR KIWI INTO IT.

...BUT IT'S BASICALLY A SIMPLE DISH.

IT TASTES REALLY GOOD...

HEY!

TSUMUGI, WANNA HELP?

WE'RE GOING TO MAKE THE PATTIES FOR THE MEAT.

YOU LIKE CLAY, RIGHT?

HEY...

WHAT WOULD CHEER YOU UP, TSUMUGI?

NO...

...AND I DIDN'T GIVE IT BACK.

I'M NOT A THIEF...

BUT THEY GAVE ME A LOT OF CLAY...

TSU-MUGI?

SO...

...DOES THAT MAKE ME A BAD GIRL?

Huh?

HEE HEE.

SO NOW...

...WE KNEAD AND KNEAD AND KNEAD...

ぱちんっ
SLAP
AND THEN FORM IT INTO A PATTY LIKE SO...
ぱちんっ
SLAP
...WHILE GETTING THE AIR OUT.
コクリ。
NOD
OKAY! COME ON, TSUMUGI!
MMPH!
ぱ
SMACK!
んっ

SIZZLE

We're stewing it after it's fried, so it just needs to change color!

Hmm...

Is the other side cooking, too?

STEAM
STEAM
STEAM

Carefully...

Carefully...

Crumble a bouillon cube with your fingers...

DROP
DROP

Ooh!

We can make a simple sauce with canned tomatoes as the base! ♪

Let's add ketchup and tonkatsu sauce!

IT'S ANOTHER BIG SUCCESS!

It's...

HEY! WE'RE PRETTY GOOD AT THIS, AREN'T WE?

It's good!

Hee

IT'S SO LIGHT AND FLUFFY!

I'M GLAD.

YUP.

Hee hee hee!

I'M SORRY.

DADDY'S BIRTHDAY PRESENT!

OH, RIGHT!

WHAT WERE YOU TRYING TO MAKE WITH ALL THAT CLAY, TSUMUGI-CHAN?

Chapter 3 – END

The Promised SALISBURY STEAK

One sunny-side up egg for each person!

☆ Ingredients ☆ Serves 3-4

Fry up the rest and eat it!

300 g mixed ground pork
and beef

1 onion

1/2 egg

4 Tbsp bread crumbs

2 Tbsp milk

1/2 tsp salt

dash of pepper

1 Tbsp olive oil

Sauce

(A) 1 clove garlic (minced)   2 bay leaves   1 400 g can diced tomatoes

(B) 1/2 tsp salt   dash of pepper

Steps

1. Mince the **onion** and cook it thoroughly in the **olive oil** until translucent, then
take it out and let cool.
Soak the **breadcrumbs** in the **milk**.
Beat the **egg**.

This stuff

2. Put the **meat** into a bowl and mix with **salt** and **pepper** until combined.
Add the ingredients from **Step 1** (reserving half of the onion) and mix until it
starts to stick together.

PAT PAT

3. Divide what you made in **Step 2** into three or four portions and
toss them between your hands to help the meat bind. Shape into
patties and make a little depression in the middle using your finger.

4. Using the frying pan from **Step 1**, cook the patties from **3**. (If it's not a
non-stick frying pan, put down some oil.) Cook on medium heat.
Onion juices! Once both sides are browned, remove and put on a plate.

5. Add a small amount of **olive oil** to the frying pan from **Step 4**. Add sauce
ingredients A and cook on low heat. Once they start to smell good, put in the
rest of the **onions** from **Step 1** and the **canned tomatoes**. Add the ingredients
from **B** and stew for about 5 minutes. Then return the patties to the pan,
cover, and stew for 7 minutes.

6. Take out the **bay leaves**, then reduce the sauce, stirring occasionally so
it doesn't burn.

♡ Top with the sunny-side eggs you cooked ahead of time. ♡

You can add bouillon cubes, ketchup,
or oyster sauce to the sauce.

Mix in part of the egg when you eat it! ♡

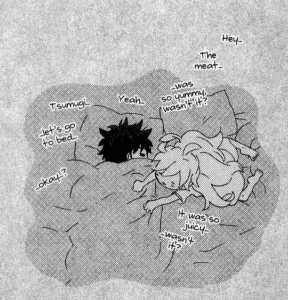

IN THAT TIME, WE'RE GOING TO MAKE ONIGIRI, FRIED CHICKEN, TAMAGOYAKI, CABBAGE AND SHIRASU STIR-FRY, MARINATED VEGETABLES, HAM SKEWERS, CHIKUWA STUFFED WITH CUCUMBER AND CHEESE, AND SQUASH AND CREAM CHEESE!

WE'VE GOT ABOUT THREE HOURS UNTIL YOU GUYS LEAVE AND I MEET WITH MY MOM.

LET'S DO OUR BEST!

UH...

All that?

OKAY, FOR STARTERS...

...LET'S MAKE THE MARINATED (?) VEGGIE THINGIES.

THE WHAT NOW?

YOU SOAK WHATEVER VEGGIES YOU LIKE IN SWEET 'N' SOUR STUFF.

CUCUMBERS

TURNIPS

CARROTS

LETTUCE

CELERY

THIS IS MY CHANCE TO MAKE UP FOR WHEN SHE SKIPPED OUT ON FLOWER-VIEWING!

OF COURSE!

YOU'RE REALLY FIRED UP!

YOU WATCH US!

WHAT DO I DO?

117

...IF I MAKE A REALLY DELICIOUS LUNCH, SHE'LL BE SO SURPRISED!

SO...

YOUR MOM'S REALLY BUSY, ISN'T SHE?

THAT'S RIGHT. I HAVEN'T HAD TIME TO REALLY TALK TO HER LATELY.

I can't show her how much better I've gotten at cooking.

I BET SHE'LL BE REALLY HAPPY.

SHE *WILL* BE SURPRISED.

YOU'RE RIGHT.

FRIED CHICKEN?

AND NOW WE START THE FRIED CHICKEN...

THEN WE DRAIN AND MARINATE THE VEGETABLES.

IF YOU DON'T MIND, WRITE DOWN WHAT YOU PUT IN AND HOW MUCH.

So we can make it again later.

I'M TASTE-TESTING EVERY-THING, OKAY?

Wow.

FRIED CHICKEN!

FRIED CHICKEN!

LET'S EAT IT!

THE FRIED CHICK-EN?

I LOVE FRIED CHICKEN!

YES. WE MARINATE IT IN A SAUCE WITH GARLIC, GRATED GINGER, SAKE, AND LOTS OF SOY SAUCE, AND THEN...

ONCE IT SOAKS UP THE FLAVOR, WE FRY IT!

WOOOOW

W-WE'RE MAKING THE FRIED CHICKEN LATER...

Huff
Huff

I WANNA MAKE FRIED CHICKEN, TOO!

But I wanna... but I wanna!

uhh...

Right, right.

OKAY, TSUMUGI.

CAN YOU MAKE THE HAM AND CARROTS 'N' STUFF INTO STARS WITH THIS?

HM MM?

YOU CAN LAYER VEGGIES WITH HAM OR WHATEVER AND THEN STICK A TOOTHPICK THROUGH THEM TO MAKE THEM CUTE!

They sell all kinds of cute ones.

WOW!

YES!!

YOU'RE THE GIRL FOR THE JOB!

WE'RE COUNTING ON YOU!

YAY!

I DID THAT LAST TIME!

OH, THAT...

GRIP''

UM... COAT THE PAN WITH SESAME OIL, TOSS IN THE CABBAGE AND SHIRASU...

BUSY

OH, THIS! LET'S MAKE THIS!

UMM... UM... UM...!

BUSY It needs to absorb water.

Pace

Pace

The rice isn't quite done yet—

For little under an hour, maybe?

WE NEED TO LET THE FRIED CHICKEN MARI- NATE.

121

CABBAGE AND SHIRASU STIR-FRY

DONABE RICE WITH KONBU STOCK

MICRO-WAVED SQUASH WITH CREAM CHEESE

CHIKUWA STUFFED WITH CUCUMBER AND CHEESE

WOULDN'T IT HAVE BEEN EASIER TO CUT THE CHIKUWA AFTER WE PUT THIS STUFF IN?

Oh!

HAM AND VEGGIE STACKS (WITH MAYO)

ah

WHEW

UNTIL NOW, WE'VE BEEN CUTTING, MIXING, AND OCCASIONALLY SAUTEEING THINGS...

...WHICH IS STUFF WE CAN DO AT OUR LEVEL.

BUT... FRIED STUFF IS AT THE TOP OF THE PYRAMID, ISN'T IT?

I know!

THIS IS WHERE IT GETS ROUGH, ISN'T IT?

Slicing fish and stuff

Frying things

Hard

Ingredients you've never heard of

Seasonal stuff

Easy

Microwaving

Just add hot water

Their idea of difficult cooking.

ピー"

SQUEAK

OOH...

WE'VE GOT ALL THAT DONE.

THREE LEFT, YEAH.

THREE LEFT?

Onigiri
Fried chicken
Tamagoyaki
Cabbage
Shir...

I JUST NEED TO MAKE SOMETHING OMELETTE-ISH RIGHT?

HUH?

Huh?

SENSEI! YOU'RE AMAZING!

OH, BUT...

...I CAN MAKE TAMAGO-YAKI.

I think...

TAMAGOYAKI IS WHEN YOU PILE A BUNCH OF THIN, THIN LAYERS OF EGG ON TOP OF EACH OTHER!

I KNOW!

SENSEI, THAT'S NOT...

CLATTER

IT'S SWEET!

Y-YOU'RE ABSOLUTELY RIGHT.

PAT PAT

THAT'S WHAT TAMAGOYAKI IS, RIGHT?

...

LOOKS LIKE YOU'RE NOT GETTING OUT OF IT, SENSEI. HEH HEH.

Heh heh

I THINK THAT...

...HAVING SEEN HOW HARD YOU WORKED TO MAKE IT...

...SHE WON'T CARE IF IT'S GOOD OR NOT.

SHE'LL BE HAPPY.

Ha ha

Heh...

AT LEAST, I WOULD BE IF I WERE HER.

THANK YOU...

I, UH...

OKAY.

...BUT IF I HAD A DAD, MAYBE THIS IS WHAT HE'D BE LIKE.

I DON'T KNOW...

OKAY, BETTER GET READY FOR THIS, TSUMUGI!

THREE EGGS.

A TEASPOON OF SUGAR.

SALT... IN YOU GO!

CRACK

CLENCH

Easy now, keep it thin...

Ooh...

YOU'RE GOOD AT THIS, SENSEI!

FRSH

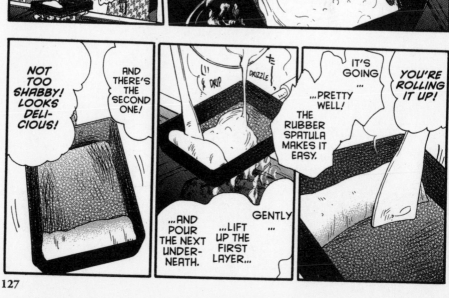

NOT TOO SHABBY! LOOKS DELICIOUS!

AND THERE'S THE SECOND ONE!

DRIP

DRIZZLE

...AND POUR THE NEXT UNDERNEATH.

GENTLY...

...LIFT UP THE FIRST LAYER...

IT'S GOING ...PRETTY WELL! THE RUBBER SPATULA MAKES IT EASY.

YOU'RE ROLLING IT UP!

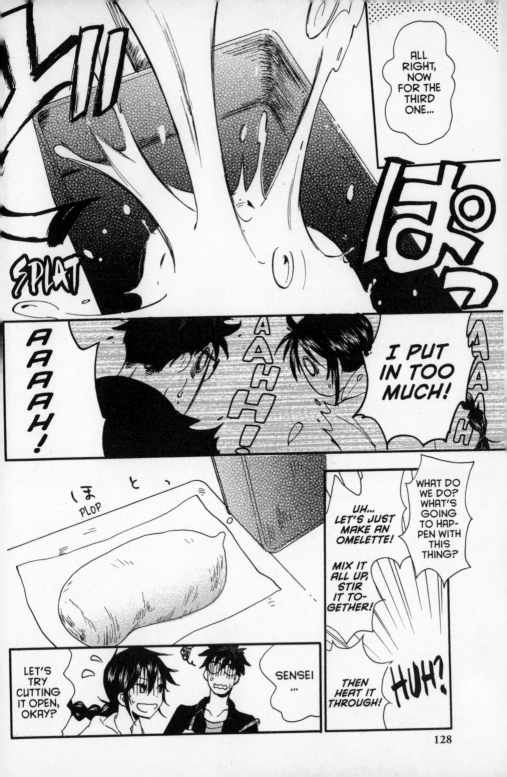

ALL RIGHT, NOW FOR THE THIRD ONE...

SPLAT

AAAAH!

AAHH!

I PUT IN TOO MUCH!

PLOP

WHAT DO WE DO? WHAT'S GOING TO HAPPEN WITH THIS THING?

UH... LET'S JUST MAKE AN OMELETTE!

MIX IT ALL UP, STIR IT TO-GETHER!

HUH?

THEN HEAT IT THROUGH!

LET'S TRY CUTTING IT OPEN, OKAY?

SENSEI ...

CRUNCH
さく

は
CHOMP

CHEW!

OH.

TASTE TEST, PLEASE.

I WISH I'D DONE IT WITH HIM.

WHEW!

YUP!

YUP!

...WHILE THEY'RE STILL WARM.

STEP
ぱた

Oh. I'LL MIX THEM...

...WITH THE SWEET 'N' SPICY SAUCE...

STEP
ぱた

I'M SO GLAD...

YUP! JUST YOU WAIT!

WAS THE FRIED CHICKEN A SUCCESS?

THE FRIED CHICKEN GOES HERE.

IT'S A FRIED CHICKEN FARM!

SAME WITH THE CHIKUWA!

'CAUSE IT'S WHITE?

YUP!

HEAVEN'S UP ABOVE, SO THAT'S WHERE YOU PUT THE EGGS!

SNEAKING A BITE IS THE BEST PART OF PACKING LUNCH!

I'M GONNA DO IT, TOO!

THERE'S ONE LEFT OVER.

CHOMP

ARE YOU ALLOWED TO DO THAT?

IS THAT OKAY?!

CHEW

Heh heh.

OH.

HI, MOM!

YEAH, I JUST GOT DONE MAKING IT.

RING RING

Just a bite, just a bite...

MAKE SURE YOU LEAVE ENOUGH TO EAT LATER!

Ah!

YEAH.

YEAH.

I SEE.

IT'S FINE. YOU CAN'T HELP IT.

ARE YOU GONNA BE OKAY?

ARE YOU GETTING ENOUGH SLEEP? ARE YOU SURE YOU'RE NOT WORKING TOO MUCH?

I DON'T WANT YOU COLLAPSING, OKAY?

CAN YOU DO ME A FAVOR?

SO, SENSEI.

YUP. SHE SKIPPED OUT ON ME AGAIN!

UM... WAS THAT...?

...YEAH.

BYE.

SNAP

I'LL EAT THIS WITH MY MOM WHEN SHE COMES BACK TONIGHT.

I'M FINE.

NO, IT'S FINE.

THANKS! I'LL SEND THIS TO MY MOM!

IT'S FINE, BUT...

...ARE YOU OKAY?

PLIP

!

POURRRR

PLIP

PLIP

...

...SAID IT'D BE CLEAR.

WAH ?!

NO WAY! THE WEATHER REPORT...

TSU-MUGI...

I'M SORRY, TSUMUGI.

...

WOW!

WHAT THE HECK?

IT'S DELI-CIOUS!

RISE

...

CHEW

I'll ask her about it.

HUH? THE CABBAGE AND SHIRASU TASTES REALLY... BLAND.

I THINK MOM'S IS BETTER.

I MADE THE RICE FIRMER TODAY, AND IT'S REALLY GOOD.

WOW! IT'S SO GOOD!

THE TAMAGO-YAKI TURNED OUT JUST FINE!

I'M GLAD THE MARINADE DIDN'T GET TOO SALTY.

WHAT A GREAT GOLDEN WEEK.

WE MADE ALL THIS...

...BY OUR-SELVES.

CLATTER

...CAN WE...

SO...

...EAT HERE?

Huh?

SEN-SEI?!

WHAT HAPP...

Oh, wow...

RAIN?!

POUR

THAT'S RIGHT. IT'S RAINING.

YES.

はっ POP

ふぃ

IT'S JUST A NAPTIME TOY.

WOW!

A TENT!

I'm glad I brought it.

WOW!

W...

Sorry to put it up on your tatami mats...

No, it's perfectly fine.

Sweet and Spicy
⟍⟍ FRIED CHICKEN ⟍⟍

☆ Ingredients ☆ Serves 3-4

300 g chicken (thighs)   cold water
a little potato starch   1/2 Tbsp white sesame seeds

(A) 3 Tbsp soy sauce   2 Tbsp sake
    1 tsp grated ginger   1 tsp minced garlic

(B) 2 Tbsp soy sauce   1 Tbsp sugar   1 Tbsp mirin

Meat!   ! Steps !

1. Cut **chicken** into bite-sized chunks and soak in **cold water** for 10 minutes.

2. Take the **chicken** out of the water and gently pat dry.
   Mix the ingredients listed in **A** and marinate **chicken** for 10 minutes.

3. Lightly coat the **chicken** with **potato starch** and fry at 160° C for a minute and a half. When the surface turns light brown, take the pieces out and let them rest for 3 minutes. Increase the oil temperature to 190° C and fry again for 40 seconds.

Hmm_

Wow_

If it really starts bubbling it's about 190 degrees C.

Note: Stick cooking chopsticks in and if small bubbles start forming near the tip, it's about 160° C.

4. Put all the ingredients listed in **B** into a saucepan and mix. Place the pan on medium heat. Once it boils down, add the **white sesame seeds.**

5. Pour 4 evenly over 3.

It makes you want some rice, doesn't it?

⋅ POINT ⋅
Pour the sauce on while the chicken is hot!

CONVERSION NOTES:
300 G CHICKEN = ABOUT 10 1/2 OZ, 160° C = 320° F, 190° C = 375° F

DAZE

IF YOU'RE THAT INTERESTED IN HER, ASK HER TO JOIN US!

YEAH, ASK HER YOUR-SELF.

Oh, look.

IIDA-SAN'S FROZEN STILL.

CLATTER

B-BUT SHE'S ALWAYS EATING SOMETHING DURING BREAKS.

SHE DOESN'T SEEM TO BE EMBARRASSED ABOUT EATING ALONE. MAYBE THAT'S JUST HER POLICY OR SOMETHING...

Feel better soon!

Take care!

HEFT

SHE'S HOT...

IT'S BEEN A YEAR SINCE THE LAST TIME SHE GOT SICK.

WHY DIDN'T I...

...NOTICE THIS MORNING?

RECEPTION

IS THAT WHY?

AH!

GOLDEN WEEK

THAT'S WHAT YOU DO, RIGHT?

CHANGE HER PJS.

LET HER SWEAT A LOT.

MAKE SURE SHE'S WARM.

PLENTY OF WATER.

PACE

PACE

Wheeze

TSUMUGI GOT SICK, AND...

YEAH, IT'S KŌHEI.

OH, MOM?

RING RING

CLICK

...

YES, THANK YOU!

I SHOULD MAKE SURE SHE'S WARM, AND SWEATS A LOT, AND GETS PLENTY OF WATER, RIGHT?

YEAH!

I WENT TO THE DOCTOR ALREADY!

BYE.

YEAH, YOU TOO.

CLICK

DOOOOOT

ARE HER KNEES OKAY? MAKE SURE SHE USES HER CANE.

IT'S FINE. YOU'VE GOT GRANNIE TO TAKE CARE OF.

YES.

YOU, TOO.

Ha ha.

PAT

TSUMUGI.

Sigh...

SHAKE

SHAKE

YOU COULDN'T EAT YOUR LUNCH, RIGHT? ARE YOU HUNGRY?

HOW IS YOUR STOMACH FEELING?

THE SPECIAL...

OKAY. IF THERE'S ANYTHING YOU WANT TO EAT, LET ME KNOW.

...

OKAY. I'LL BUY IT... ...WHEN I GO GET DINNER.

I was in such a hurry.

RIGHT... I SHOULD'VE BOUGHT IT.

HUH? OH! OH! RIGHT, RIGHT! THE SPECIAL!

DING DONG!

UGH...

Huff

Wheeze

ARE YOU GOING SOME-WHERE?

...

SNIFFLE

They moved to the living room.

IS HER TEMPERATURE HIGH?

Hee hee...

ARE YOU OKAY? DO YOU FEEL ALL RIGHT?

YES?

KO-TORI-CHAN!

DADDY SAID I COULD WATCH MAGI-GAL.

SURE THING. WANT ME TO PUT IT IN?

WHIRR

Magi

Magi!

AS LONG AS I HAVE THESE STRONG FEELINGS AND A HEART THAT BELIEVES...

I WON'T GIVE UP!

...MY WISH WILL COME TRUE!

THAT'S MOMMY.

BA-DUMP

THAT'S RIGHT!

HEH HEH!

WE WERE ALREADY FRIENDS!

I see!

I THOUGHT MAYBE IT WOULD MAKE YOU FEEL A LITTLE LESS LONELY...

?

I THOUGHT YOU WERE ALREADY MY FRIEND.

Huh?

I BOUGHT IT!

Huff

Huff

Welcome back!

Oh!

DADDY'S BACK!

I'M BACK!

CAN: WHITE PEACHES

白桃

THE "YOU GOT A COLD" SPECIAL...

Mmph

はっ
JUMP

AAAH

SLURP

Yay!

ZZZ...

She ate it all.

GO BACK TO BED.

Oh... STAGGER
ふらふら

STAGGER

I'M ALL BETTER NOW...

Heh heh.

WHEN I GOT COLDS, I USED TO EAT CANNED PEACHES, TOO.

FOR ME, IT WAS ALWAYS APPLE SAUCE.

I SEE.

BUT WHAT'S BREAD PORRIDGE?

I HAD RICE PORRIDGE AND SOFT UDON NOODLES.

Hmm...

IT'S NICE TO HAVE A SPECIAL MEAL YOU ONLY EAT WHEN YOU'RE SICK.

Ah

AND THERE WAS VEGGIE SOUP AND BREAD PORRIDGE...

COLD CHAWANMUSHI...

YOU TEAR UP SOME BREAD AND SIMMER IT IN MILK 'TIL IT GETS SOUPY.

NOT AT ALL. THANKS FOR YOUR HELP.

Oh.

...I'M SORRY I'VE STAYED SO LONG...

OH!

You add in sugar or honey to make it sweet.

Ahh... it's so delicious.

UH...

UM...

...

164

IF YOU'RE GOING TO MAKE SOME-THING, DO YOU WANT ME TO HELP?

Whew

THAT WOULD BE SUCH A HUGE HELP!

Oh!

RIGHT!

WE NEED TO ASK HER FIRST.

I THINK WE CAN MAKE THAT.

LET'S ASK TSUMUGI-CHAN IF THERE'S ANYTHING SHE WANTS TO EAT.

I'M SO GLAD!

OKAY, WHAT SHOULD WE MAKE?

Hmm...

I'M INTERESTED IN THIS BREAD PORRIDGE STUFF. RICE PORRIDGE IS EASY. OR WE COULD ALSO DO UDON...OR CHAWANMUSHI LIKE YOU MENTIONED.

Hmm?

What ingredients do you have on hand?

Um, this and this and this...

166

PACKAGES: KONBU (TOP), KATSUO (BOTTOM)

KONBU

KATSUO BUSHI

For the dashi stock

KAMABOKO

EGGS

For the chawan-mushi

FU

CLUTTER

MITSBA

For the nyuumen

SOMEN NOODLES from last summer

CARROTS

DAI-KON

GREEN ONIONS

WE CAN DO IT!

LET'S GET STARTED!

...AND PUT IT ON MEDIUM HEAT.

YOU PUT THE KONBU IN THE WATER...

Don't put the lid on.

CLICK

One 10 cm square piece or so per liter.

Huh?

REMEMBER THAT, OKAY?

AT MY HOUSE...

...WE MAKE DASHI FROM KONBU AND KATSUO-BUSHI.

We're making it?

SHF

BOX: INSTANT DASHI

BUBBLE

THEN TAKE OUT...

...THE KONBU BEFORE IT BOILS.

BUBBLE

ONCE IT STARTS TO SINK, YOU TURN OFF THE HEAT.

CLICK カチ

Then add lots of katsuo-bushi.

BUBBLE ふ

あ

さ

THEN YOU WAIT FOR IT TO SINK ALL THE WAY...

...TO THE BOT-TOM.

MAYBE THAT'S WHY I'M EXCITED NOW.

IT WAS ALWAYS SO EXCITING!

BUT WHEN I WAS A KID, I USED TO LOVE WATCHING MY MOM MAKE IT.

THIS IS ACTUALLY THE FIRST TIME I'M MAKING MY OWN STOCK.

Heh!

YOU LOOK REALLY EXCITED.

HUH?

168

IT'S REALLY PURE.

IT'S LIKE...

IT... IT'S GOOD...

REALLY?

!

THE FIRST THING WE'LL USE THIS DASHI FOR IS THE CHAWANMUSHI!

Oh! I GUESS I REALLY CAN'T TELL. I'M SORRY.

I've never understood the difference between the store-bought ones, either.

Ugh.

But it feels like it would be good for you.

I...I'll cut up the mitsuba.

Okay.

Mix it carefully so you don't get bubbles...

Pour the dashi, soy sauce, sake, and salt through a strainer when you add it.

Beat the eggs.

THIS IS EXCITING!

Now, before you pour the red liquid in...

...AND CHECK OUT THIS KAMA-BOKO!

Heh heh!

OOH!

SLICED MAGI-GAL KAMABOKO

STRAIN THE EGG MIXTURE...

Put either aluminum foil or a cloth napkin on top.

...give it two minutes on high, then 15-20ish on low.

AH...

Like this.

DON'T WORRY. YOU CAN USE A POT.

Fill the water to a third of the way up the chawan cups.

Once it starts boiling...

YOU DON'T HAVE A STEAMER, DO YOU?

(Yes, he does)

HMM... PROBABLY NOT?

THAT'S FINE.

SORRY, I'M LEAVING THAT TO YOU.

I SHOULD CUT THE VEGGIES FIRST, RIGHT?

...WHILE IT'S STEAM-ING.

LET'S GET THE NYUU-MEN READY...

SO LEAVE IT TO ME.

CHOP

I'VE BEEN...

...STARTING TO REALLY LIKE IT.

CHOP

CHOP

CHOP

RIGHT!

But let's add mirin and soy sauce.

OOH... IT LOOKS DELICIOUS ALREADY...

WHEN SHOULD WE COOK THE SOMEN NOODLES?

OH, I WANT TO COOL THE CHAWAN-MUSHI FIRST.

BUBBLE

BUBBLE

...HARDER VEGETA-BLES INTO THE STOCK FIRST.

PUT THE...

MOMMY
...

IT'S A PAIN TO DO. I THINK YOU'RE FINE USING THE STORE-BOUGHT STUFF.

Well...

IT TAKES TIME, BUT YOU REALLY CAN MAKE YOUR OWN STOCK, HUH?

TOSS

SO-MEN NOO-DLES

BUT...

...IT DOESN'T HURT TO KNOW HOW TO MAKE IT.

Then why did we...?

HUH?

FOR SOME REASON...

...I REALLY WANTED YOU TO GO FOR IT TODAY...

...TO BE EVEN NICER THAN USUAL...

...TO TSUMUGI-CHAN.

WHAT IS IT?

RUB
むちゃー

THAT SMELLS GOOD.

NO, IT WAS YOU!

HEY!

YOU'RE THE ONE WHO DID ALL THE WORK TODAY.

Huh?

IT'S DINNER!

GOBBLE
GOBBLE

IT'S SO
GOOD...

OF COURSE THERE WAS.

I guess I'm an older guy now.

Ooh! THERE WAS A TIME WHEN YOU WERE IN HIGH SCHOOL?

SLICE

SLIDE

I USED TO EAT THIS FOR A LATE-NIGHT SNACK IN HIGH SCHOOL ALL THE TIME.

THIS BRINGS BACK SO MANY MEMORIES.

Salt water

HUH?

But the apples are still...

CLICK

TSUMUGI-CHAN, FEEL BETTER!

I... I'M GOING HOME!

IF...

THANKS SO MUCH.

Ha ha!

THE APPLES! ADD A LITTLE OF THAT ORANGE JUICE IN THE FRIDGE AND THEY'LL LOOK GOOD AND TASTE GOOD!

Oh!

ARE YOU OKAY?

TAKE CARE...

Chapter 5 – END

CHAWANMUSHI

❗ Dashi Stock

☆ Ingredients ☆ Serves 3-4

1 L water
40 g katsuobushi
10 cm sq piece konbu

Maybe we'll use home-made next time.

For the pork miso soup, we used store-bought stock.

Steps

1. Put the **water** and **konbu** into a stockpot on medium heat, and take out the **konbu** just before it boils.

2. Add the **katsuobushi** to the pot. Once the **katsuobushi** starts to sink, turn off the heat and remove scum from the stock's surface. Once the katsuobushi completely sinks, strain it gently.

✱**POINT** If you squeeze the **katsuobushi** while straining, the dashi won't taste right, so be careful!

❗ Chawanmushi

☆ Ingredients ☆ Serves 3-4

Tastes great hot or chilled!

3 eggs   kamaboko, mitsuba to taste

Ⓐ 450 cc dashi stock (3x the amount of eggs)
1 tsp soy sauce   1 tsp sake
1 scant tsp salt

❤**POINT** You can add whatever else you want: shrimp, chicken, shiitake mushrooms, lily bulbs, gingko nuts, etc.

Steps

1. Beat the **eggs**, making sure that bubbles don't form. Add the ingredients from **A**. Mix carefully and then strain!

2. Cut the **kamaboko** into bite-sized pieces. Place a couple in the bottom of each dish before pouring in the egg mix from **step 1**. Cover each cup with aluminum foil.

3. Fill a big pot with water, about one third of the height of the cups, and heat. When the water boils, put the cups from **step 2** into the pot. Put the lid on the pot loosely, and after 2 minutes turn to low heat.

4. After the cups steam for 15-20 minutes, remove and place **mitsuba** on the egg surface. Reseal with aluminum foil and let steam a little longer.

CONVERSION NOTES:
1 L WATER = ABOUT 4 1/4 CUPS, 40 G KATSUOBUSHI = ABOUT 1.5 OZ, 10 CM KONBU = 4 IN., 450 CC DASHI = 2 CUPS

Plain chawanmushi is still good.

LET'S MAKE OUR HIGH SCHOOL DEBUT!

It's Almost Time for High School

YOU LOOK PRETTY GOOD, SO IF YOU CAN JUST GET RID OF THE GLASSES...

...YOU'LL BE A LOT EASIER TO APPROACH AND MAKE LOTS OF FRIENDS!

I don't think I need to do that.

SIGNS: A REAL OPTOMETRIST (TOP), WE HAVE CONTACTS (BOTTOM)

Huh?

BUN: MEAT

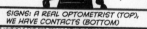

SO THIS IS IT, HUH?

RUMBLE

ちゃんとした 眼科

コンタクトするよ

Yay!

Okay.

SHE'S REALLY THINKING ABOUT ME.

Come on, let's be super-popular together!

SHOULD WEAR A BLAZER IN HIGH SCHOOL, BUT HERE SHE'S SHOWN WEARING A SAILOR UNIFORM, DUE TO AUTHORIAL PREFERENCE.

181

SIGN: EYE

YOU CAN DO IT, KOTORI...!

OKAY.

FIRST WE'LL EXAMINE YOUR EYES TO SEE IF YOU'RE OKAY TO WEAR CONTACT LENSES.

I'M SUPPOSED TO PUT THESE IN MY EYES?!

THEY'RE PRETTY BIG...

STUNNED

Here.

LET'S TRY PUTTING THEM IN.

HMM... YOU'RE JUST FINE.

huff

huff

OKAY!

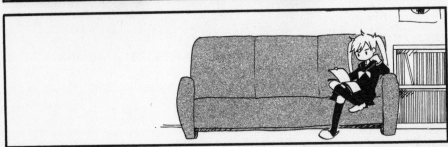

Hyah...

HYAAAHH!

No way no way no way!

WELL...

That was so scary.

Waaahhhh!

LET ME THINK ABOUT IT...

Come back soon!

...IF YOU REALLY DON'T WANT TO, YOU DON'T HAVE TO DO IT.

I'LL BUY YOU SOME NICE RAMEN, SO CHEER UP.

おいしい ラーメン

中華

SIGNS: YUMMY RAMEN (TOP), CHINESE (BOTTOM)

Really?

Yeah.

The 380 yen one. The cheapest they have.

183

STEAM

TA-DA!

SCARF

SLURP SLURP
SLURP SLURP

SLURP
SLURP
SLURP

MAYBE I'LL TRY THOSE CONTACTS, AFTER ALL.

Oh?

BLURRY

RUB
RUB

The End

184

Afterword

See you next volume!

雨隠 ギド
Gido Amagakure

Thank you!

Koz, Gon-chan, Tsuru-san, W-yama-san

O-hara-san, M-chan, E-san, Nori-chan

T-shiro-sama, Jun Abe-sama
Research Support: Tabegoto-ya Norabo-sama
Cooking Advisor: Yo Tatewaki-sama

Thank you for all for your help!!

Translation Notes

Flower viewing, page 10: Flower viewing refers to Hanami, the Japanese tradition of viewing flowers in full bloom. Though this may include any type of flower, it mostly refers to cherry blossoms and, less often, plum blossoms. Hanami is typically done in spring and is often enjoyed as a picnic-like activity where friends, family, and coworkers eat prepared meals while observing the beauty of flowers in bloom.

Donabe, page 26: A special type of clay pot used for cooking over an open flame.

Nozawana, miso beef, and iwanori seaweed, page 39: Nozawana is a type of Japanese mustard leaf that if often pickled. Miso beef or *nikumiso* is a mixture of ground beef and miso. Iwanori (rock seaweed) is a type of seaweed found between rocks that is typically dried for consumption. All three of these foods are typically used as condiments or rice toppings.

The role of a teacher, page 54: In Japan, the role of a teacher can sometimes be a little different from that of their Western counterparts. Japanese teachers may be more directly involved in the life of students inside and outside school, almost functioning as second parents. Though there is a clearer line between teacher and student these days, in the past, the student-teacher relationship was much more intimate, and it wasn't uncommon for teachers to spend time with their students and their students' families outside of school.

Thumbprint, page 56: Though signing one's name has become fairly common in Japan, ink stamps/seals and thumbprints are still used to sign documents.

Salisbury steak, page 58: In Japan, this dish is called *hanbaagu* or may also be called hamburg steak. *Hanbaagu* is a standard of *yoshoku* (Western-style cooking) and you'll find some version of it in almost every *famiresu* (family-style restaurant) in Japan.

Konnyaku, page 59: A starchy plant also known as "devil's tongue." It's made into a gelatin form and used as an ingredient in Japanese dishes.

Golden Week, page 113: In early May, a series of holidays form a week of vacation, allowing many students and families to travel or spend time together.

Shirasu, page 117: Dried baby anchovies.

Chikuwa, page 117: A tube-shaped food product made from fish paste, starch, and other ingredients.

Konbu, page 122: A type of thick kelp that is often dried and used in the preparation of soup stock.

Tatami mats, page 140: A type of traditional Japanese flooring typically made of rice straw.

Chawanmushi, page 164: A savory, steamed egg custard eaten as a main dish in Japan. Chawanmushi directly translates to "steamed (in) tea bowl" and the dish itself is traditionally served in a tea bowl.

Nyuumen, page 166: Thin wheat-flour noodles in a broth with vegetables, meat, and any number of other ingredients.

Katsuobushi, page 167: Dried, fermented skipjack tuna that is typically shaved off into flakes. It is also used to prepare soup stock.

Kamaboko, page 171: A type of processed fish paste primarily made from pureed whitefish and formed into a loaf that can be sliced i.

Disaster strikes...

...the nuzuka House-hold.

...

BLECH

Tsumugi doesn't want to eat her green peppers.

AHH!

Uh huh.

The dinner table freezes.

Daddy will do his best so that Tsumugi can enjoy her veggies!!

A gratin filled with veggies.

Will it work?

Will Tsumugi smile...

...and say it's delicious?

甘々と稲妻 Sweetness & Lightning 2

On Sale September 2016!

NO.6

A PERFECT LIFE
IN A PERFECT CITY

For Shion, an elite student in the technologically sophisticated city No. 6, life is carefully choreographed. One fateful day, he takes a misstep, sheltering a fugitive his age from a typhoon. Helping this boy throws Shion's life down a path to discovering the appalling secrets behind the "perfection" of No. 6.

KC
KODANSHA
COMICS

Praise for the anime:

"The show provides a pleasant window on the highs and lows of young love with two young people who are first timers at the real thing."

-The Fandom Post

"Always it is smarter, more poetic, more touching, just plain better than you think it is going to be."

-Anime News Network

Say I Love You.

KC KODANSHA COMICS

Mei Tachibana has no friends — and says she doesn't need them!

But everything changes when she accidentally roundhouse kicks the most popular boy in school! However, Yamato Kurosawa isn't angry in the slightest—in fact, he thinks his ordinary life could use an unusual girl like Mei. But winning Mei's trust will be a tough task. How long will she refuse to say, "I love you"?

a Silent Voice

KC
KODANSHA
COMICS

Shoya is a bully. When Shoko, a girl who can't hear, enters his elementary school class, she becomes their favorite target, and Shoya and his friends goad each other into devising new tortures for her. But the children's cruelty goes too far. Shoko is forced to leave the school, and Shoya ends up shouldering all the blame. Six years later, the two meet again. Can Shoya make up for his past mistakes, or is it too late?

Available now in print and digitally!

SWAPPED WITH A KISS?!

Class troublemaker Ryu Yamada is already having a bad day when he stumbles down a staircase along with star student Urara Shiraishi. When he wakes up, he realizes they have switched bodies—and that Ryu has the power to trade places with anyone just by kissing them! Ryu and Urara take full advantage of the situation to improve their lives, but with such an oddly amazing power, just how long will they be able to keep their secret under wraps?

Available now in print and digitally!

A Kodansha Comics Trade Paperback Original.

Published in the United States by Kodansha Comics,
an imprint of Kodansha USA Publishing, LLC, New York.

Publication rights for this English edition arranged through Kodansha Ltd.,
Tokyo.

First published in Japan in 2013 by Kodansha Ltd., Tokyo, as *Ama-ama to
Inadzuma* volume 1.

ISBN 978-1-63236-456-2

Printed in the United States of America.

www.kodanshacomics.com

9 8 7 6 5 4 3 2 1

Translation: Adam Lensenmayer
Lettering: Lys Blakeslee
Editing: Ajani Oloye
Kodansha Comics Edition Cover Design: Phil Balsman